**2**

# LET'S GO

### 4th Edition

STUDENT BOOK

R. Nakata

K. Frazier

B. Hoskins

C. Graham

OXFORD

UNIVERSITY PRESS

UNIVERSITY PRESS

198 Madison Avenue
New York, NY 10016 USA

Great Clarendon Street, Oxford, OX2 6DP, United Kingdom

Oxford University Press is a department of the University of Oxford.
It furthers the University's objective of excellence in research, scholarship,
and education by publishing worldwide. Oxford is a registered trade
mark of Oxford University Press in the UK and in certain other countries

© Oxford University Press 2012

The moral rights of the author have been asserted

First published in 2012

2016 2015 2014 2013 2012

10 9 8 7 6 5 4 3 2 1

**No unauthorized photocopying**

General Manager, American ELT: Laura Pearson
Executive Publishing Manager: Shelagh Speers
Senior Managing Editor: Anne Stribling
Project Editor: June Schwartz
Art, Design, and Production Director: Susan Sanguily
Design Manager: Lisa Donovan
Designer: Sangeeta E. Ramcharan
Electronic Production Manager: Julie Armstrong
Production Artist: Elissa Santos
Image Manager: Trisha Masterson
Image Editor: Joe Kassner
Production Coordinator: Hila Ratzabi
Senior Manufacturing Controller: Eve Wong

ISBN: 978 0 19 462619 4 Student Book with Audio CD
ISBN: 978 0 19 464307 8 Student Book as pack component
ISBN: 978 0 19 464361 0 Audio CD as pack component

Printed in China

This book is printed on paper from certified and well-managed sources

ACKNOWLEDGEMENTS

*The authors and publisher are grateful to those who have given permission to reproduce
the following extracts and adaptations of copyright material:*

*Illustrations by*: Bernard Adnet: 57, 75; Ilias Arahovitis: 8(t), 20(t), 42(t), 52(t),
53(t); Fian Arroyo: 27(t), 63(t); Jared Beckstrand; 24(t), 38, 62(t), 68(t); Reginald
Butler: 50(t), 51, 56(b); Donna Catanese: 7, 25, 34(t), 61, 69, 74; Terri & Joe
Chicko: 6(t); Lawrence Christmas: 39; Chi Chung: 9(b), 17, 35(b), 45(b), 63(b);
Garry Colby: 21; Bob Depew: 44(t), 45(t); Marion Eldridge: 64, 65; Kathi Ember:
18, 19; Ken Gamage: 9(t); Jesse Graber: 13(b), 26(t), 27(b), 31, 35(t), 72, 73;
Daniel Griffo: cats on pages 4, 6, 8, 10, 12, 14, 16, 18, 21, 22, 24, 26, 28, 30, 32,
34, 36, 40, 42, 44, 46, 48, 50, 52, 54, 58, 60, 62, 64, 66, 68, 70 and 72; Sharon
Harmer: 49(t); Diane Hays: 10, 11; Richard Hoit: 5(b), 23(b), 41, 53(b), 59, 60(t),
70(t), 71(b); Colleen Madden: 54, 55; Katie McDee: 36, 37; Shawn McKelvey:
14(t); Marc Mones/AA Reps Inc.: 32(t), 33, 56(t), 71(t); Sherry Rogers: 15, 20(b),
49(b), 67; Dan Sharp: 2, 3, 4, 5(t), 6(b), 8(b), 12, 14(b), 16(b), 22, 23(t), 24(b), 26(b),
30, 32(b), 34(b), 40, 42(b), 44(b), 48, 50(b), 52(b), 58, 60(b), 62(b), 66, 68(b), 70(b),
Janet Skiles: 13(t), 16(t); Ken Spengler: 28, 29, 46, 47; Christopher Wurth: 43.

*Text Design*: Molly K. Scanlon
*Cover Design*: Susan Sanguily
*Cover Illustrator*: Daniel Griffo

# Table of Contents

Kate

Andy

Jenny

Scott

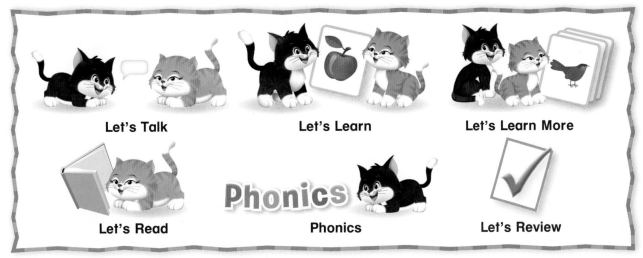

Let's Talk

Let's Learn

Let's Learn More

Let's Read

Phonics

Let's Review

# Let's Remember

## Let's Talk

**A** **Listen and say.** (CD1 03)

(CD1 04)

| How about you? | Good-bye! |
|---|---|
| I'm OK. | See you later! |
| Pretty good! | |

I am = I'm

## B Listen and sing.

# The Hello and Good-Bye Song

Hi, Scott. How are you?
　I'm fine, thank you.
Hi, Jenny. How are you?
　Pretty good, thank you.
Hi, Andy. How are you?
　OK, thank you.
Hi, Kate. How are you?
　I'm fine.

Good-bye, Scott.
　See you later, alligator!
Good-bye, Jenny.
　See you later, alligator!
Good-bye, Andy.
　See you later,
　See you later.
See you later, alligator!
Good-bye, Kate!

## C Say and act. Say hello and good-bye.

Hi, _____. How are you?

I'm _____. How about you?

_____!

Good-bye, _____!

See you later!

# Let's Learn

## A Learn the words. CD1 06

1. a picture

2. a window

3. a pencil sharpener

4. a workbook

5. a paper clip

6. a clock

7. a door

8. a calendar

## B Ask and answer. CD1 07

What's this?

It's a picture.

What's that?

It's a window.

CD1 08

| What's this? It's a picture. | What's that? It's a window. | It is = It's What is = What's |
| --- | --- | --- |

**6 Unit 1** At School

# C Ask and answer. CD1 09

this

that

CD1 10

| Is | this<br>that | a calendar? | Yes, it is.<br>No, it isn't. |
|---|---|---|---|

is not = isn't

# D Listen, point, and chant. CD1 11

## What's This? What's That?

What's this?

What's that?

   This is a spider.

   That's a cat.

What's this?

What's that?

   This is a baseball.

   That's a bat.

This is a spider.

That's a cat.

This is a baseball.

That's a bat.

# Let's Learn More

## A Learn the words. CD1 12

1. paper clips

2. pictures

3. clocks

4. workbooks

5. calendars

6. pencil sharpeners

7. windows

8. doors

## B Ask and answer. CD1 13

What are these?

They're paper clips.

What are those?

They're pictures.

 CD1 14

| What are these? | What are those? |
|---|---|
| They're paper clips. | They're pictures. |

They are = They're

**8 Unit 1** At School

## C Play a game. Ask your partner.

| Are | these those | doors? | Yes, they are. No, they aren't. |
|---|---|---|---|

are not = aren't

## D Listen and do. CD1 16

1. Point to the clock.

2. Touch the picture.

3. Write your name.

4. Sharpen your pencil.

## Phonics

A B C D E F G H I J K L **M** N O P Q R S T U V W X Y Z
a b c d e f g h i j k l **m n** o p q r s t u v w x y z

## A Listen, point, and say.  CD1 17

# Mm

mop

map

mug

# Nn

notebook

nine

nut

## B Listen, point, and chant.  CD1 18

### The M N Phonics Chant

Hop on the **m**op,
Not the broom.
I **n**eed the **n**ame
Of the **m**an in the **m**oon.

# What Do You See?

**1**

What's that?
What do you see?
There's a man with a mop.

**2**

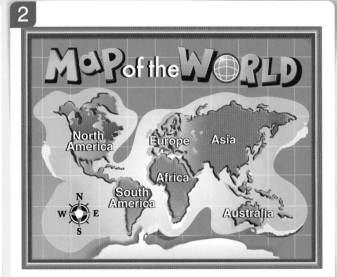

What are those?
What do you see?
There are names on the map.

**3**

What's this?
What do you see?
There's a nut on my notebook.

**4**

What are these?
What do you see?
There are nine names on mugs.

# Unit 2 My Things

## Let's Talk

CD1 21

Whose bag is that?
It's Jenny's bag. It's her bag.
It's Scott's bag. It's his bag.

Jenny's = her
Scott's = his

## B Listen and sing. CD1 22 ♪♫

# Whose Bag Is That?

Whose bag is that?
   I don't know.
Is it Scott's bag?
   No, no, no.
   It isn't his bag.
   No, it isn't.
   No, it isn't Scott's bag.

Is it Jenny's bag?
   Yes, it is.
   It's her bag.
   Yes, it is.
   It isn't his bag.
   It's her bag.
   It isn't Scott's bag.

## C Say and act. Ask your friend.

Whose bag is that?
Is it _____'s bag?

No, it isn't _____ bag.

Is it _____'s bag?

Yes, it's _____ bag.

# Let's Learn

## A Learn the words. CD1 23

   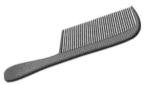

1. a key      2. a candy bar      3. a comic book      4. a comb

  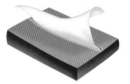 

5. a coin      6. a brush      7. a tissue      8. a watch

## B Ask and answer. CD1 24

What do you have?

I have a key.

CD1 25

What do you have?
I have a key.

14    **Unit 2** My Things

# C Play a game. CD1 26

| Do you have a key?<br>Yes, I do. | Do you have a tissue?<br>No, I don't. |
| --- | --- |

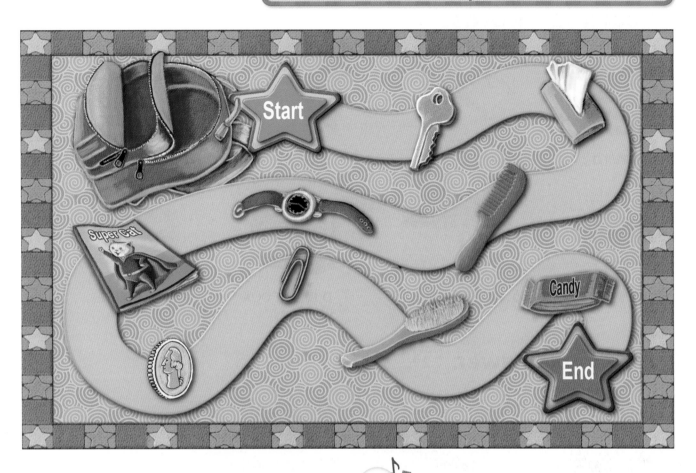

# D Listen, point, and chant. CD1 27

## What Do You Have in Your Bag?

What do you have in your bag?
Look and see.
I have books! One, two, three.
One for you, and two for me.
I have books! One, two, three.

What do you have in your bag?
Look and see.
I have candy bars! One, two, three.
One for you, and two for me.
I have candy bars! One, two, three.

# Let's Learn More

## A Learn the words. CD1 28

 1. a camera

 2. a key chain

 3. a music player

 4. a calculator

 5. a train pass

6. an umbrella

 7. a lunch box

 8. a wallet

## B Ask and answer. CD1 29

What does he have?

He has a wallet.

What does she have?

She has a key chain.

CD1 30

| What does | he<br>she | have? | He<br>She | has a wallet. |
| --- | --- | --- | --- | --- |

## C Ask your partner. (CD1 31)

(CD1 32)

Does she have an umbrella?
Yes, she does.
No, she doesn't.

## D Listen and do. (CD1 33)

1. Listen to music.

2. Eat lunch.

3. Buy a comic book.

4. Take a picture.

**Phonics**

A B C D E **F** G H I J K L M N O P Q R S T U **V** W X Y Z

a b c d e **f** g h i j k l m n o p q r s t u **v** w x y z

**A Listen, point, and say.**  CD1 34

Ff  5

fan          five          fork

Vv

van          vest          violin

**B Listen, point, and chant.** CD1 35

## The F V Phonics Chant

The fox feels fine
On his visit to the van.
The van's very hot.
The fox loves the fan.

# Making Music

**1**

This is a man.
He has a vest.
He feels fine.

**2**

What's that?
It's a van with a fan.

**3**

What's in the van?
There's one violin.

**4**

Look! There are five violins
and five vests!

# Let's Review ✓

## A Listen and check. (CD1 37)

1.

A ☐   B ☐   C ☐

2.

A ☐   B ☐   C ☐

3.

A ☐   B ☐   C ☐

4.

A ☐   B ☐   C ☐

5.

A ☐   B ☐   C ☐

6.

A ☐   B ☐   C ☐

7.

A ☐   B ☐

8.

A ☐   B ☐

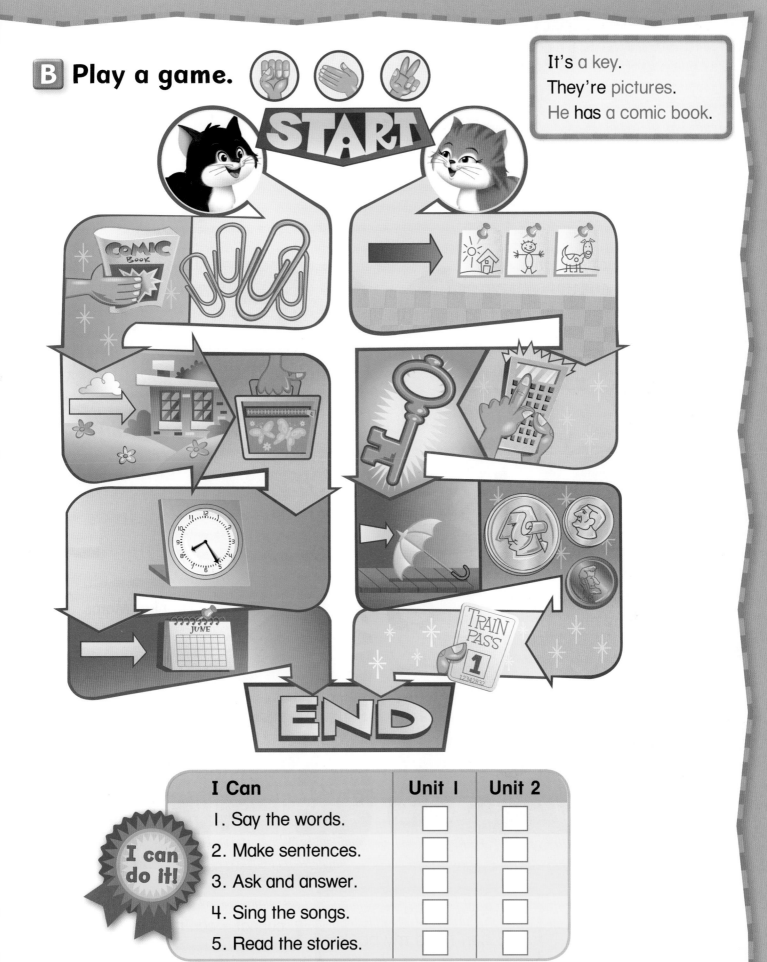

**B Play a game.**

It's a key.
They're pictures.
He **has** a comic book.

| I Can | Unit 1 | Unit 2 |
|---|---|---|
| 1. Say the words. | ☐ | ☐ |
| 2. Make sentences. | ☐ | ☐ |
| 3. Ask and answer. | ☐ | ☐ |
| 4. Sing the songs. | ☐ | ☐ |
| 5. Read the stories. | ☐ | ☐ |

I can do it!

**A** **Listen and say.** CD1 38

CD1 39

What's wrong?
I can't find my **book**.

cannot = can't

## B Listen and sing.

### What's Wrong?

What's wrong, Andy?
  I can't find my book.
What's wrong, Andy?
  I can't find my book.

I can't hear the teacher.
I can't reach the bookshelf.
I can't find my pencil.
I can't see the board.
Oh, Andy!

He can't hear the teacher.
He can't reach the bookshelf.
He can't find his pencil.
He can't see the board.

## C Say and act. Ask your friend.

What's wrong, _____?

Is it in your _____?

I can't find my _____.

I don't know.

Oh, here it is. It's in my _____. Thanks!

# Let's Learn

## A Learn the words.

1. ride a pony

2. play the piano

3. do a magic trick

4. play hopscotch

5. play with a yo-yo

6. do a cartwheel

7. do a somersault

8. jump rope

## B Make sentences.

Look at him!
He can do a magic trick.

Look at her!
She can play the piano.

| Look at | him! her! | He She | can do a magic trick. |

## C Ask and answer. CD1 44

1.
2.
3.
4.

CD1 45

What can she do?
She can jump rope.

## D Listen, point, and chant. CD1 46

### Look at Me!

Look at me.
I can climb a tree.
Look at me.
Look at me.

Look at me.
I can climb a tree.
Look at me.
Look at me.

Look at him. He can swim.
Look at him. He can swim.

Look at her. She can run.
Look at her. She can run.

Look at me.
I can climb a tree.
Look at me.
Look at me.

# Let's Learn More

## A Learn the words. (CD1 47)

1. dance

2. swim

3. run

4. sing

5. skip

6. read

7. paint

8. color

## B Make sentences. (CD1 48)

They can read.

(CD1 49)  They can read.

**26 Unit 3** Things I Can Do

## C Play a game. Ask your partner. (CD1 50)

Can they skip?
Yes, they can.
No, they can't.

## D Listen and do. (CD1 51)

1. Play baseball.

2. Ride a bicycle.

3. Use chopsticks.

Hello!

4. Speak English.

## Phonics

A B C D E F G H I J K L M N O P Q R S T U V W X Y Z

a b c d e f g h i j k l m n o p q r s t u v w x y z

**A** Listen, point, and say. CD1 52

**Ll**

long

little

like

**Rr**

run

race

ride

**B** Listen, point, and chant. CD1 53

## The L R Phonics Chant

The lion runs like the rabbit.

He loves to race at night.

Lions really love to run,

And stop at the red light.

# What Can You Do?

1

Can you run a long race?
No, I can't.

2

They can run.
They like long races.

3

What about you?
What can you do?

4

I can ride a little unicycle.
Yes, I can. Look at me!

## Let's Talk

**A** **Listen and say.** CD1 55

CD1 56
I hope you feel better soon.
Thanks.

## B Listen and sing. CD1 57 ♪♫♪

### What's the Matter?

What's the matter?
What's the matter?
What's the matter?
I am sick.

What's the matter?
Are you OK?
 I am sick today.
Oh, no!

hot    cold    tired    sad

## C Say and act. What's the matter?

What's the matter, _____?

I'm _____.

That's too bad.
 I hope you feel better soon.

_____.

# Let's Learn

## A Learn the words. (CD1 58)

1. a cook

2. a nurse

3. a taxi driver

4. a doctor

5. a police officer

6. a teacher

7. a student

8. a farmer

## B Make sentences. (CD1 59)

He's a cook.

She's a teacher.

Occupations

CD1 60

| He's | a cook. |
| She's | |

He is = He's
She is = She's

32  **Unit 4** Occupations

CD1 62

> Who's he?
> He's a student.

> Who is = Who's

**D** Listen, point, and chant. CD1 63

## Is He a Teacher?

| | |
|---|---|
| Is he a teacher? | Is he a farmer? |
| Yes, he is. | No, he isn't. |
| Is she a student? | Is she a cook? |
| Yes, she is. | No, she isn't. |
| Are they nurses? | Are they teachers? |
| No, they aren't. | No, they aren't. |
| They're doctors. | They're students. |

# Let's Learn More

## A Learn the words. CD1 64

1. pilots

2. salesclerks

3. office workers

4. engineers

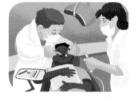
5. dentists

6. firefighters

7. teachers

8. students

## B Ask and answer. CD1 65

Who are they?

They're office workers.

CD1 66

Who are they?
They're office workers.

34    **Unit 4** Occupations

# C Ask and answer. (CD1 67)

Are they dentists?
Yes, they are.   No, they aren't.

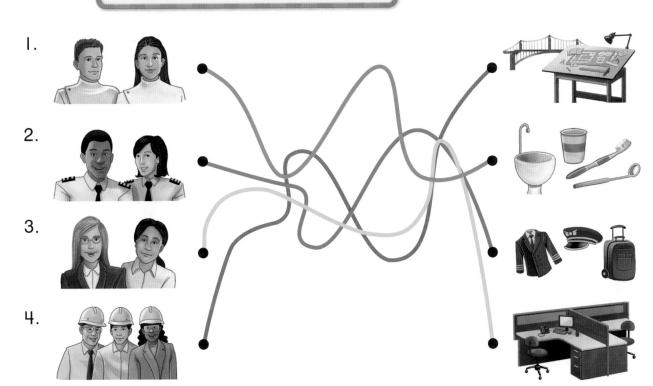

1.
2.
3.
4.

# D Listen and do. (CD1 69)

1. Drive a taxi.

2. Use a computer.

3. Fly a plane.

4. Climb a ladder.

# Phonics

ABCDEFGHIJKLMNOPQRSTUVWXYZ
abcdefghijklmnopqrstuvwxyz

**A** Listen, point, and say. CD1 70

## a_e        ai        ay

game        make        paint        rain        play        today

**B** Listen, point, and chant. CD1 71

## The Long A Phonics Chant

Play today!
Paint the rain.
Make a cake.
Paint a wave.

# A Rainy Day

**1**

Oh, no! Look at the rain.
We can't play today.

**2**

I can make a cake.
I'm a cook!

**3**

Let's play a game.
No, let's paint.

**4**

I can paint pictures.
Look at my pictures!

# Let's Review ✓

## A  Listen and check.  CD1 73

1.

A ☐   B ☐   C ☐

2.

A ☐   B ☐   C ☐

3.

A ☐   B ☐   C ☐

4.

A ☐   B ☐   C ☐

5.

A ☐   B ☐   C ☐

6.

A ☐   B ☐   C ☐

7.

A ☐   B ☐

8.

A ☐   B ☐

**B** Play a game.

| I Can | Unit 3 | Unit 4 |
|---|---|---|
| 1. Say the words. | ☐ | ☐ |
| 2. Make sentences. | ☐ | ☐ |
| 3. Ask and answer. | ☐ | ☐ |
| 4. Sing the songs. | ☐ | ☐ |
| 5. Read the stories. | ☐ | ☐ |

I can do it!

# Unit 5 Things to Eat
## Let's Talk

**A** Listen and say. CD2 02

What's for lunch, Mom?

Spaghetti.

Mmm. That's good. I like spaghetti.

I do, too.

Do you want spaghetti?

Yes, please.

No, thank you!

CD2 03

Do you want spaghetti?
  Yes, please.
  No, thank you!

## B Listen and sing. CD2 04 🎵

### The Spaghetti Song

Do you like spaghetti?

Yes, I do.

I do, too.

I do, too.

Do you like spaghetti?

Yes, I do.

I like spaghetti, too!

Do you want spaghetti?

Yes, I do.

I do, too.

I do, too.

Do you want spaghetti?

Yes, I do.

I want spaghetti, too!

## C Say and act. Talk about food.

What's for lunch?

_____.

Do you want _____?

_____.

# Let's Learn

## A Learn the words. CD2 05

1. an omelet

2. a peach

3. a pear

4. a pancake

5. yogurt

6. cereal

7. tea

8. hot chocolate

## B Ask and answer. CD2 06

What does she want?

She wants a peach.

 CD2 07

What does she want?
She wants a peach.

# C Play a game. CD2 08

Does he want cereal?
Yes, he does.    No, he doesn't.

# D Listen, point, and chant. CD2 09 ♪♫♪

## Hungry Boy Chant

What does he want?

What does he want?

   Listen carefully.

   He wants

   One egg,

   Two bananas,

   Three pancakes,

Four milk shakes,

Five cookies,

   Six sandwiches.

   He's a hungry boy.

   He's a very hungry boy.

He's a hungry boy.

He's a very hungry boy.

# Let's Learn More

## A Learn the words.

1. grapes
2. pancakes
3. peaches
4. hamburgers

5. stew
6. cheese
7. pasta
8. steak

## B Ask and answer. CD2 11

What does she like?

She likes pancakes.

CD2 12

What does she like?
She likes pancakes.

44 **Unit 5** Things to Eat

(CD2 14)

Does he like steak?
Yes, he does.
No, he doesn't.

## D Listen and do. (CD2 15)

1. Count the grapes.

2. Eat a hamburger.

3. Make pancakes.

4. Peel peaches.

# Let's Read

## Phonics

A B C D E F G H I J K L M N O P Q R S T U V W X Y Z
a b c d e f g h i j k l m n o p q r s t u v w x y z

**A** Listen, point, and say. (CD2 16)

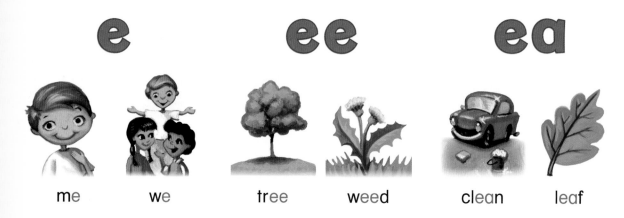

# e          ee          ea

me     we          tree     weed          clean     leaf

**B** Listen, point, and chant. (CD2 17)

## The Long E Phonics Chant

He eats weeds.
So does she.
She loves weeds.
Not me!

# Weeds and Trees

1

We like trees.
We don't like weeds.

2

Look at me!
I have a green and yellow leaf.

3

Look at the park.
It's clean!

4

I'm hungry.
Can we eat weeds?

**A Listen and say.** (CD2 19)

Where do you live, Jenny?

I live in Hillsdale.

What's your address?

It's 6 North Street.

What's your cell phone number?

It's (798) 555-2143.

| CD2 20 | Where do you live? <br> I live in Hillsdale. | What's your address? <br> It's 6 North Street. |
| --- | --- | --- |

## B Listen and sing.

### Hillsdale

Where do you live?

In Hillsdale.

Where do you live?

In Hillsdale.

I live in Hillsdale.

How about you?

I live in Hillsdale, too.

What's your address

in Hillsdale?

What's your address

in Hillsdale?

It's North Street.

Number forty-two.

I live next to you!

## C Say and act. Tell where you live.

Where do you live?

I live in _____.

What's your address?

It's _____.

# Let's Learn

## A Learn the words. CD2 22

1. a bed     2. a bathtub     3. a sofa     4. a stove

5. a lamp     6. a sink     7. a TV     8. a refrigerator

## B Ask and answer. CD2 23

Where's the workbook?

It's under the bed.

Where's the key chain?

It's by the stove.

CD2 24

Where's the workbook?
It's under the bed.

Where is = Where's

| in | under |
|----|-------|
| on | by |

**50**   Unit 6 My House

## C Make sentences. (CD2 25)

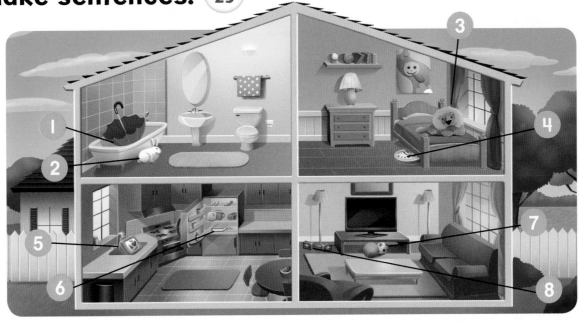

There's an umbrella in **the** bathtub.
There are balls under **the** TV.

There is = There's

## D Listen, point, and chant. (CD2 27) ♪♫

# Are There Books in the Bathtub?

Are there books in the bathtub?

No, there aren't.

Are there books in the sink?

No, there aren't.

Are there books in the refrigerator?

No, there aren't.

No, there aren't.

No, there aren't.

Is there a bird on the bed?

Yes, there is.

Is there a spider on the sofa?

Yes, there is.

Is there a baby in the bathtub?

Yes, there is.

Yes, there is.

Yes, there is.

# Let's Learn More

## A Learn the words. (CD2 28)

1. next to

2. in front of

3. behind

## B Make sentences. (CD2 29)

There's a table in front of the sofa.

(CD2 30) There's a **table** in front of **the sofa.**

# C Play a game. Ask your partner. (CD2 31)

> Is there a stove next to the sink?
> Yes, there is.
> No, there isn't.

| | |
|---|---|
| in | in front of |
| on | behind |
| under | next to |

# D Listen and do. (CD2 32)

1. Wash the dishes.

2. Take a bath.

3. Clean the room.

4. Make the bed.

# Let's Read

## Phonics

ABCDEFGHIJKLMNOPQRSTUVWXYZ
abcdefghijklmnopqrstuvwxyz

**A** Listen, point, and say. CD2 33

i_e      y      i

kite    ride      fly    my      climb    find

**B** Listen, point, and chant. CD2 34

### The Long I Phonics Chant

I like to fly my kite.
    I like to ride my bike.
I don't like bikes. I like to hike.
    I hate to hike. I like bikes.

# Save that Kite!

What's wrong?
I can't find my kite.

Look! There are five kites
in the tree.
My kite is red and white.

Cat, please climb this tree.
My kite is red and white.
Grab that line!

Thank you, Cat!
Now I can fly my kite!

# Let's Review

## A Listen and check. (CD2 36)

1.  A ☐   B ☐   C ☐

2.  A ☐   B ☐   C ☐

3.  A ☐   B ☐   C ☐

4.  A ☐   B ☐  C ☐

5.  A ☐   B ☐

6.  A ☐   B ☐

## B Listen and number. (CD2 37)

**C** **Play a game.**
**Make sentences.**

> The yogurt is by the bowl.

> He's a police officer.

| I Can | Unit 5 | Unit 6 |
|---|---|---|
| 1. Say the words. | ☐ | ☐ |
| 2. Make sentences. | ☐ | ☐ |
| 3. Ask and answer. | ☐ | ☐ |
| 4. Sing the songs. | ☐ | ☐ |
| 5. Read the stories. | ☐ | ☐ |

I can
do it!

# Unit 7 Routines

## Let's Talk

What time is it?

It's six o'clock.
It's time for dinner.

What time is it?

It's seven o'clock.
It's time for your bath, Scott.

OK.

Is it time for bed?

Yes, it is.

Good night, Mom.

CD2 39

What time is it?
It's six o'clock.

**58** Unit 7 Routines

# What Time Is It?

What time is it?

It's eight o'clock.

It's time for school. Let's go!

Come on, let's go!

It's time for school.

It's eight o'clock. Let's go!

What time is it?

It's twelve o'clock.

It's time for lunch. Let's go!

Come on, let's go!

It's time for lunch.

It's twelve o'clock. Let's go!

What time is it?

It's nine o'clock.

It's time for bed. Let's go!

Come on, let's go!

It's time for bed.

It's nine o'clock. Let's go!

**C** Say and act. Tell time.

What time is it?

It's _____.
It's time for _____.

# Let's Learn

## A  Learn the words.  CD2 41

1. get up

2. brush my teeth

3. wash my face

4. comb my hair

5. get dressed

6. eat breakfast

## B  Ask and answer.  CD2 42

What do you do in the morning?

I eat breakfast.

 CD2 43

What do you do in the morning?
I eat breakfast.

# C Ask and answer. (CD2 44)

1.
2.
3.

4.
5.
6.

(CD2 45)
Do you wash your face in the afternoon?
　　Yes, I do.
　　No, I don't.

# D Listen, point, and chant. (CD2 46)

## What Do You Do in the Morning?

What do you do in the morning?
What do you do in the morning?
What do you do?
What do you do?
What do you do in the morning?

What do you do?
I brush my teeth.
What do you do?
I wash my face.

I get up and brush my teeth,
Wash my face, and comb my hair.
I get up and brush my teeth,
Wash my face, and comb my hair.

What do you do?
I comb my hair.
I comb my hair
　in the morning.

# Let's Learn More

## A Learn the words. CD2 47

1. eat dinner

2. talk on the phone

3. do homework

4. take a bath

5. watch TV

6. study English

## B Ask and answer. CD2 48

What does he do in the evening?

He watches TV.

Scott | 1 | 2
Jenny | 3 | 4
Maria | 5 | 6

CD2 49

What does he do in the evening?
He watches TV.

| watches | does |
| takes | studies |
| talks | eats |

# C Play a game. Ask your partner. (CD2 50)

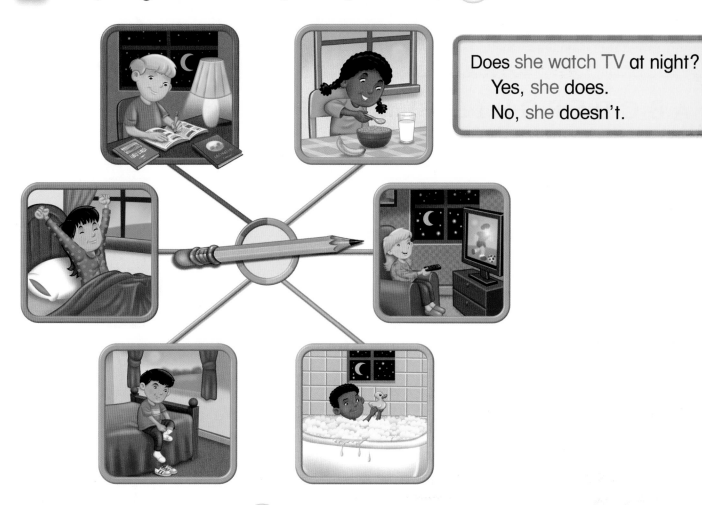

Does she watch TV at night?
Yes, she does.
No, she doesn't.

# D Listen and do. (CD2 51)

1. Play the violin.

2. Take a shower.

3. Play video games.

4. Go to bed.

## Phonics

**A B C D E F G H I J K L M N O P Q R S T U V W X Y Z**

**a b c d e f g h i j k l m n o p q r s t u v w x y z**

### A Listen, point, and say. (CD2 52)

# o_e          oa          ow

home     rope          goat     oats          bowl     grow

### B Listen, point, and chant. (CD2 53)

## The Long O Phonics Chant

My **goat** loves **oa**ts,

Chicken b**o**nes,

R**o**ses in a b**ow**l,

And ice cream c**o**nes.

# A Day on the Farm

1. This is my home. I live on a farm. Where do you live?

2. The goats eat oats in the morning. What do you eat?

3. I grow peaches. Do you eat peaches in the afternoon? Yes, we do!

4. Can we ride the pony? Yes. Hold the rope.

## Let's Talk

**A** Listen and say. (CD2 55)

Let's play a game!

What are you doing?

I'm riding a bicycle.

What are you doing?

We're swimming.

(CD2 56)

What are you doing?
  I'm riding a bicycle.
  We're swimming.

We are = We're

## B Listen and sing. CD2 57

# What Are You Doing?

What are you doing?
I'm playing a game.
Watch what I do,
And then do the same.

Clap your hands.
Count to three.
Wiggle your toes.
Smile at me.

Nod your head.
Bend your knees.
Stamp your feet.
Now say "Please."

Snap your fingers
Climb a tree.
Raise your arm.
Wave at me.

## C Say and act. Play a guessing game.

What are you doing?

I'm _____.

What are you doing?

We're _____.

# Let's Learn

## A  Learn the words. CD2 58

1. dancing

2. swimming

3. sleeping

4. drawing

5. singing

6. running

7. walking

8. reading

## B  Ask and answer. CD2 59

What's he doing?

He's drawing.

CD2 60

What's he doing?
He's drawing.

68    Unit 8  Doing Things

## C Ask and answer.  61

1.
2.
3.

4.
5.
6.

 CD2 62

Is she swimming?
Yes, she is.
No, she isn't.

## D Listen, point, and sing. CD2 63

# Doing Things

What's he doing?
  Reading.
  He's reading,
  He's reading.
What's he reading?
  He's reading a comic
  book and talking on
  the telephone.

What's she doing?
  Eating.
  She's eating,
  She's eating.
What's she eating?
  She's eating spaghetti
  and talking on
  the telephone.

What are you doing?
  Cooking.
  I'm cooking,
  I'm cooking.
What are you cooking?
  I'm cooking breakfast
  and talking on
  the telephone.

# Let's Learn More

## A Learn the words. CD2 64

1. at home

2. at school

3. at the park

4. at the store

5. at the library

6. at the zoo

## B Ask and answer. CD2 65

Where is Kate?

She's at the library.

CD2 66

Where is Kate?
She's at the library.

# C Play a game. Ask your partner.  CD2 67

| Where is he? | What's he doing? |
|---|---|
| He's at the park. | He's playing baseball. |

study → studying    buy → buying
eat → eating    take → taking

# D Listen and do. CD2 68

1. Snap your fingers.

2. Stamp your feet.

3. Open your mouth.

4. Close your eyes.

**Phonics**

A B C D E F G H I J K L M N O P Q R S T U V W X Y Z
a b c d e f g h i j k l m n o p q r s t u v w x y z

## A Listen, point, and say. CD2 69

# u_e

huge

tube

# ue

blue

glue

# ew

few        new

## B Listen, point, and chant. CD2 70 ♪

### The Long U Phonics Chant

My mule is cute.
Her name is June.
She loves sugar cubes
And new blue balloons.

# Making Art

Do you have glue?
Yes, I do. It's new.

Is that blue?
Yes, it is. I like blue.

Do you have a few tubes?
No, I don't. Ask Sue.

Look at it.
It's huge! It's singing!

# Let's Review ✓

## A Listen and check. (CD2 72)

1.

A ☐    B ☐    C ☐

2.

A ☐    B ☐    C ☐

3.

A ☐    B ☐    C ☐

4.

A ☐    B ☐    C ☐

5.

A ☐    B ☐    C ☐

6.

A ☐    B ☐    C ☐

7.

A ☐    B ☐

8.

A ☐    B ☐

**74  Units 7 and 8** Review

## B Play a game.

jump → jumping
skip → skipping
do → doing
watch → watching

Is he jumping?

Yes, he is.

**I can do it!**

| I Can | Unit 7 | Unit 8 |
|---|---|---|
| 1. Say the words. | ☐ | ☐ |
| 2. Make sentences. | ☐ | ☐ |
| 3. Ask and answer. | ☐ | ☐ |
| 4. Sing the songs. | ☐ | ☐ |
| 5. Read the stories. | ☐ | ☐ |

# Let's Go 2 Syllabus

## Unit 1 At School

| Let's Talk | Let's Learn | Let's Learn More | Let's Read |
| --- | --- | --- | --- |
| **Conversation:** How are you? I'm OK. How about you? Pretty good! Good-bye. See you later!<br><br>**Song:** The Hello and Good-Bye Song | **School Items:** a picture, a window, a pencil sharpener, a workbook, a paper clip, a clock, a door, a calendar<br><br>**Language:** What's this/that? It's a picture. Is this/that a calendar?<br><br>**Chant:** What's This? What's That? | **School Items:** paper clips, pictures, clocks, workbooks, calendars, pencil sharpeners, windows, doors<br><br>**Language:** What are these/those? They're paper clips.<br><br>**Listen and do:** point, touch, write, sharpen | **Phonics**<br><br>**Mm**<br>mop, map, mug<br><br>**Nn**<br>notebook, nine, nut<br><br>**The MN Phonics Chant**<br><br>**Story:** What Do You See? |

## Unit 2 My Things

| Let's Talk | Let's Learn | Let's Learn More | Let's Read |
| --- | --- | --- | --- |
| **Conversation:** Whose bag is that? Is it Scott's bag? No, it isn't his bag. Is it Jenny's bag? Yes, it's her bag.<br><br>**Song:** Whose Bag Is That? | **Things:** a key, a candy bar, a comic book, a comb, a coin, a brush, a tissue, a watch<br><br>**Language:** What do you have? I have a key. Do you have a tissue?<br><br>**Chant:** What Do You Have in Your Bag? | **More Things:** a camera, a key chain, a music player, a calculator, a train pass, an umbrella, a lunch box, a wallet<br><br>**Language:** What does he/she have? He/She has a wallet. Does he/she have an umbrella?<br><br>**Listen and do:** listen, eat, buy, take | **Phonics**<br><br>**Ff**<br>fan, five, fork<br><br>**Vv**<br>van, vest, violin<br><br>**The F V Phonics Chant**<br><br>**Story:** Making Music |

**Let's Review Units 1 and 2**

## Unit 3 Things I Can Do

| Let's Talk | Let's Learn | Let's Learn More | Let's Read |
| --- | --- | --- | --- |
| **Conversation:** What's wrong, Andy? I can't find my book. Is it in your desk? It's under my chair.<br><br>**Song:** What's Wrong? | **Actions:** ride a pony, play the piano, do a magic trick, play hopscotch, play with a yo-yo, do a cartwheel, do a somersault, jump rope<br><br>**Language:** Look at him/her. He/She can do a magic trick. What can he/she do?<br><br>**Chant:** Look at Me! | **Actions:** dance, swim, run, sing, skip, read, paint, color<br><br>**Language:** They can read. Can they skip?<br><br>**Listen and do:** play, ride, use, speak | **Phonics**<br><br>**Ll**<br>long, little, like<br><br>**Rr**<br>run, race, ride<br><br>**The LR Phonics Chant**<br><br>**Story:** What Can You Do? |

## Unit 4 Occupations

| Let's Talk | Let's Learn | Let's Learn More | Let's Read |
| --- | --- | --- | --- |
| **Conversation:** What's the matter, Scott? I'm sick. I hope you feel better soon! Thanks.<br><br>**Song:** What's the Matter? | **Jobs:** a cook, a nurse, a taxi driver, a doctor, a police officer, a teacher, a student, a farmer<br><br>**Language:** He's/She's a cook. Who's he/she?<br><br>**Chant:** Is He a Teacher? | **Jobs:** pilots, salesclerks, office workers, engineers, dentists, firefighters, teachers, students<br><br>**Language:** Who are they? They're office workers. Are they dentists?<br><br>**Listen and do:** drive, use, fly, climb | **Phonics**<br><br>**a_e** game, make<br><br>**ai** paint, rain<br><br>**ay** play, today<br><br>**Long A Phonics Chant**<br><br>**Story:** A Rainy Day |

**Let's Review Units 3 and 4**

# Unit 5  Things to Eat

| Let's Talk | Let's Learn | Let's Learn More | Let's Read |
|---|---|---|---|
| **Conversation:** What's for lunch, Mom? Spaghetti. I like spaghetti. I do, too. Do you want spaghetti? Yes, please. No, thank you!<br><br>**Song:** The Spaghetti Song | **Food:** an omelet, a peach, a pear, a pancake, yogurt, cereal, tea, hot chocolate<br><br>**Language:** What does she want? She wants a peach. Does he want cereal?<br>**Chant:** Hungry Boy Chant | **Food:** grapes, pancakes, peaches, hamburgers, stew, cheese, pasta, steak<br><br>**Language:** What does she like? She likes pancakes. Does she like steak?<br><br>**Listen and do:** count, eat, make, peel | **Phonics**<br><br>**e** me, we<br>**ee** tree, weed<br>**ea** clean, leaf<br><br>**Long E Phonics Chant**<br>**Story:** Weeds and Trees |

# Unit 6  My House

| Let's Talk | Let's Learn | Let's Learn More | Let's Read |
|---|---|---|---|
| **Conversation:** Where do you live? I live in Hillsdale. What's your address? It's 6 North Street. What's your cell phone number? It's (798) 555-2143.<br><br>**Song:** Hillsdale | **Household Items:** a bed, a bathtub, a sofa, a stove, a lamp, a sink, a TV, a refrigerator<br><br>**Language:** Where's the workbook? It's under/by/in/on the bed.<br><br>**Chant:** Are There Books in the Bathtub? | **Locations:** next to, in front of, behind<br><br>**Language:** There's a table in front of the sofa. Is there a stove next to the sink?<br><br>**Listen and do:** wash, take, clean, make | **Phonics**<br><br>**i_e** kite, ride<br>**y** fly, my<br>**i** climb, find<br><br>**Long I Phonics Chant**<br>**Story:** Save that Kite! |

**Let's Review Units 5 and 6**

# Unit 7  Routines

| Let's Talk | Let's Learn | Let's Learn More | Let's Read |
|---|---|---|---|
| **Conversation:** What time is it? It's six o'clock. It's time for dinner. It's seven o'clock. It's time for your bath. Is it time for bed? Yes, it is. Good night, Mom.<br><br>**Song:** What Time Is It? | **Morning Routines:** get up, brush my teeth, wash my face, comb my hair, get dressed, eat breakfast<br><br>**Language:** What do you do in the morning? I eat breakfast. Do you wash your face in the afternoon?<br><br>**Chant:** What Do You Do in the Morning? | **Evening Activities:** eat dinner, talk on the phone, do homework, take a bath, watch TV, study English<br><br>**Language:** What does he do in the evening? He watches TV. Does she watch TV at night?<br><br>**Listen and do:** play, take, go | **Phonics**<br><br>**o_e** home, rope<br>**oa** goat, oats<br>**ow** bowl, grow<br><br>**Long O Phonics Chant**<br>**Story:** A Day on the Farm |

# Unit 8  Doing Things

| Let's Talk | Let's Learn | Let's Learn More | Let's Read |
|---|---|---|---|
| **Conversation:** Let's play a game! What are you doing? I'm riding a bicycle. We're swimming.<br><br>**Song:** What Are You Doing? | **Actions:** dancing, swimming, sleeping, drawing, singing, running, walking, reading<br><br>**Language:** What's he doing? He's drawing. Is she swimming?<br><br>**Song:** Doing Things | **Places:** at home, at school, at the park, at the store, at the library, at the zoo<br><br>**Language:** Where is she/he? She's/He's at the library. What's he doing? He's playing baseball.<br><br>**Listen and do:** snap, stamp, open, close | **Phonics**<br><br>**u_e** huge, tube<br>**ue** blue, glue<br>**ew** few, new<br><br>**Long U Phonics Chant**<br>**Story:** Making Art |

**Let's Review Units 7 and 8**

# Word List